Beyond *the* Busyness

An Ultimate Handbook For MSME's to Achieve Stress Free Business Growth

Beyond
the
Busyness

An Ultimate Handbook For
MSME's to Achieve Stress Free
Business Growth

GULSHAN GABA

Worldwide Published by
Pendown Press

PENDOWN PRESS LLP

An ISO 9001 & ISO 14001 Certified Co.,
Regd. Office: 3767A, Kanhaiya Nagar,
Tri Nagar, Delhi-110035
Ph.: 8130886000, 9650072927, 8595249536
E-mail: info@pendownpress.com
Branch Office: 1A/2A, 20, Hari Sadan, Ansari Road,
Daryaganj, New Delhi-110002
Ph.: 011-45794768
Website: PendownPress.com

First Edition: 2023
Price: ₹299/-
ISBN: 978-93-5554-888-7

Layout and Cover Designed by Pendown Graphics Team
Printed and Bound in India by Thomson Press India Ltd.

Dedication

To my Isht, the ultimate Guru, along
with all the Gurus, Coaches,
Grandparents, Parents, Family, Friends,
and Fellow Entrepreneurs — your
guidance, support, and inspiration have
been the foundation
of my journey. Your wisdom and
encouragement have shaped me into
who I am today.

CONTENTS

ACKNOWLEDGEMENTS

I would like to express my gratitude to many people who made an impact on me and my life and have supported me to create this book.

First and foremost, I would like to thank my parents and grandparents. They have nor only been my source of inspiration but also my lifelong teachers, instilling moral values in me. From childhood, I learned the importance of living a fulfilling life by serving the community around me.

My appreciation goes to my dedicated wife for her continuous care and support at home. Her dedication in the management of household responsibilities and upbringing of our children has allowed me to focus on writing, and I couldn't have done it without her.

I am thankful to my beloved Guru, Akshar Yadav who opened up a realm of opportunities across various aspects of my life by giving an eye-opening mantras and sutras of life, he guided me towards achieving both inner and outer success. His teachings truly transformed my way of thinking, and I owe the creation of this book entirely to him. My heartfelt thanks go to my son and daughter, whose unwavering love and support mean the world to me. Equally, I'm thankful to my brother and sister for believing in me and my endeavours.

My friends have also been a great source of encouragement, with a special shoutout to Raman Chawla for generously offering his peaceful farmhouse for the writing process. Lastly, I want to thank God for giving me the energy and clarity to write this book.

Gulshan Gaba

August 13, 2023

ABOUT THE AUTHOR

Gulshan Gaba, a Business Efficiency Expert, empowers MSME business owners to break free from daily operations complexities, allowing them to focus on key growth areas of business. He works on the development and growth of team leaders, aligning them with the Vision, Mission and Goals of the organisation.

He is also a practising Chartered Accountant having standing of more than 30 years in his profession. During the tenure of 30 years, he has provided advisory services to leading PSUs nationalised banks, listed companies and the MSME sector. His notable accomplishments are as under:

1. Chartered Accountant

2. Insolvency Professional

3. Certified Forensic Auditor

4. Certified Arbitrator

5. Certified Independent Director

6. Business Coaching India Graduate

7. Tech Mastery in Business

During the career of 30 years, he has worked with numerous big and small companies across a wide range of industries. He has not only helped them achieve their business goals but has also played a role in realizing their personal aspirations. His involvement has led to significant turnarounds in their fortunes.

He has handled various strategic business initiatives, including Strategic Financial Planning, Mergers, Demergers, Business Restructuring, Corporate Governance, and bringing in investors for business.

He is extremely committed to enhancing the financial well-being of business owners through his writings, training and quality services.

2

WHY THIS BOOK

Every entrepreneur dreams of running their business just like every big multinational company does. When an entrepreneur starts their journey of business, they do so with a passion and zeal, with a twinkle in their eyes to reach to the moon. They work so hard in their business to solve the challenges which come in the journey of entrepreneurship such as Managing cash flows & Inventories, creating niche in marketing & finding customers, handling accounts & taxes, staying competitive and tackling uncertainties.

In the pursuit of attaining their dreams, they work tirelessly, keeping themselves busy all the time. They control each and every aspect of the business so closely that they become completely absorbed by it. As the business expanded, they started delegating their works to others. However, since they lack formal training delegation and team management, the way they used to handle things leaves them in a difficult position.

As a result, they keep themselves involved in each and every aspect of business, leaving very little time for themselves and their families. The stress of the business starts taking a toll on their physical & mental health. They start getting irritated with their staff, clients and even their own family. The original purpose that initially motivated them to start their journey of business loses its steam. Gradually, the business that was meant to improve their lives begins to dominate the life of the business owner and those of their family members.

I have worked very closely with a lot of business owners throughout my career spanning more than 30 years and have witnessed their ups & downs in their journey of business. They possess a very good understanding of the market and about their products or services, but when it comes to the art of managing their people, the absence of any formal training often leads to struggles in achieving desired outcomes. This in turn, hampers their growth.

Having worked extensively in this space for many years, I have gained valuable insights into the factors that hinder the growth of business owners. I can promise you that if you follow the strategies explained in the upcoming chapters and build a strong and motivated team aligned with the goals of the organisation around you, you will not only be able to accelerate your business growth but also lead a happier, more relaxed, and stress-free life.

By not reading this book and missing out on the strategies and actions highlighted in this book, you might end up spending more time trying to achieve the growth of your business. This could lead to struggling with managing your team and firefighting all the time day-to-day crises of business, affecting your health & overall happiness.

I am on a mission to help small business owners through this book, to empower themselves to lead a relaxed and happy life, spending quality time with family and friends while also nurturing business growth through effective teamwork within a healthy and supportive environment where everyone is committed to contribute towards the success of organisation in a very cohesive, noise less & flawless business environment.

I genuinely hope you enjoy reading this book and, most importantly, it allows you to transform your organisation.

MY STORY

I, too, fell victim to this situation in my initial years of practice. In 1990, I started the journey of my dreams with full enthusiasm and unwavering zeal, fueled by a passion to serve my clients diligently. This was the time when the share market was at its peak and was giving good returns. Everyone in the country was investing in the stock market and was making money. I was also not an exception to it and started trading in shares.

As my investments started paying off, I saw an opportunity to expand. I started borrowing money from my family and friends, assuring them of minimum guaranteed returns, and invested that money in shares. Initially, my business model went very well and I was doubling my investments every six months and feeling on top of the world.

I got married in November 1991, and during that time, I was making a significant amount of money. However, a turning point arrived on the 4th day of May, 1992, when the infamous Harshad Mehta scam broke out and the share market started rolling down and suddenly all my investments went into red. I was literally on the road with huge debts and no financial support from anyone. I was shattered with no money in hand to support me and my newlywed wife at one end and the borrowings on my head at the other end, which I took from my family and friends.

Despite the challenges, I held on to my courage and decided to focus on my practice to pay off the debts. For the next five years, I worked hard, serving my clients to repay the loans. During this time, my office timings stretched from 10 am to 7 pm to 7 am to 10 pm. I was busy all the time, serving my clients. Initially, my wife supported me, considering our financial situation and the opportunities my profession brought. We enjoyed some comforts that my wife and I were deprived of in the initial years of our married life.

But as the time went on and things got better, I kept being busy in my profession all the time and it became my habit.

Once again, I found myself making money from my profession as I was sincerely and dedicatedly served to my clients. During this time, I was completely focussed on my profession. As the practice expanded, so did my time commitments, stretching me thin. Unfortunately, it started taking a toll on my health and my family also felt disturbed as I was not giving time to them. Even though I gradually increased my staff, effectively delegating tasks remained a challenge due to time limitations. I was not delegating the work effectively so that they could perform on their own but in the absence of any formal training they were dependent on me.

As I was busy in day-to-day operations, I found it challenging to bill my clients and was unable to focus on attracting new clients. As a result, my cash flows began to suffer. I started delaying the payment of the staff and other vendors, which had an adverse impact on the morale of my team. Even though I was delivering excellent services to my clients, reflecting my work execution, the business management aspect of my practice was completely disorganised. I had always believed that serving my clients should be of the highest priority, as that's what my clients require from me.

While the execution of work is important, having a well-organized, well-run business is as important as the work that my business produces.

Now the question arises: as a business leader, you can't be present in every place simultaneously. How do you concentrate on the business while ensuring that everyone is working in the business? This is why a common challenge for small businesses is effectively managing workflow, especially as your business scales. View every aspect of your business as equally important. If you don't send out bills to your clients or collect payment, your business wouldn't function. If you don't do marketing, then you won't get new customers or clients, and your excellent work won't matter. All parts of your business are as important as the work output.

Although I was doing great in my profession, I found myself without funds in my bank accounts as I was not raising bills to my clients on time. Whatever money I was generating that was barely enough to pay my office overheads and my credit card bill. I was working very hard from 7 am to 10 pm, yet I was not taking home any money. All my money was stuck with my clients as pending payments, with no proper collection system in place. I was working like a machine and it started taking a toll on physical and mental health. I was under constant stress all the time, and unfortunately, I ended up venting all my anger on my staff and family, which had negative consequences for both my personal and professional life.

In the initial years of my life, I used to be carefree and enjoy life to the fullest. However, as time went on, I became a more isolated and serious person. And I broke ties with my friends, and even my wife started avoiding me in social gatherings. My life seemed to be falling apart, and I could feel myself slowly going towards depression without any clear idea of how to resolve the current situation.

4

MY REALISATION

I will never forget the day of 12th December, 2008, when I was sitting at the Income Tax Department in New Delhi, waiting for my turn to appear in a case. Suddenly, I received a call from my mother, who was residing in Karnal, informing me that my father had been in an accident and had sustained a head injury. They'd taken him to PGI Chandigarh, and I was told to come there quickly. I reached the hospital at 9 pm that day, and I found my father lying unconscious on the bed. The doctors explained to us that he had blood clots in his brain and needed to be put on a ventilator for treatment.

The next morning, the doctors told us that there were only three ventilators, and all were already being used, but they were trying to spare one for us as a priority. At that point,

I decided to explore ventilator options in private hospitals. I found a hospital named Silver Oak in Mohali. It had 200 beds. Through some reference, I met Dr. Bhargava, who was the founder & promoter in the hospital and a doctor by profession himself. Despite the chilly winter weather, he welcomed me into his chamber, creating a warm and relaxed atmosphere.

During our conversation, he mentioned that they had a ventilator available in the ICU and suggested that we can shift the patient here. I inquired about the hospital's ICU and ventilator charges, and he provided me with details. I decided to shift my father to this hospital.

I was told to submit money at the cash counter to start the admission process, so I did that. As soon as my father arrived at the hospital, his treatment began immediately. He was taken care of very well by the receiving staff. They changed his clothes, cleaned him up, gave him a hospital gown, and then transferred him to the ICU with a lot of care..

He was there for 20 days, and every alternate day, I received a message on my phone reminding me to submit the hospital charges, which I deposited at the cash counter. On the second day, I noticed that the charges were slightly higher than what the owner had initially told me on the first day. I thought it best to discuss this with the doctor. I went to his office again for the second time. Once more, I found him in a relaxed and comfortable setting, sitting in a cozy environment. I brought up the issue of the charges, and he responded by saying that he didn't exactly remember the initial quote, but the charges that are being charged now are the actual one. He said even if he'd made a mistake and said lower fees before, they couldn't be changed now.

During those 20 days, I realised that the founder and promoter of the hospital, despite being a practising doctor himself, was not directly involved in the hospital's day-to-day operations. He was just supervising the business side of the hospital and all the processes of the hospital, be it any department were handled by his team. It is a known fact that to run a hospital effectively, apart from having qualified doctors, administrative and nursing staff, there are multiple processes and procedures that must be in place. Running a hospital is quite a complicated and tedious process.

A small mistake in treating a patient can lead to significant consequences, to the extent that the hospital might have to pay a lot of money as compensation and dent to the reputation of the hospital. But, despite all odds, every aspect and process involved in running a hospital was managed by the staff of the hospital in a smooth and flawless manner, without any noise and disturbances. From treatment and diagnostics centres to operation theatres, the canteen, admission procedures, billing, housekeeping, collections, and discharges, the hospital team handled everything exceptionally well. The owner of the hospital didn't seem bothered by all these processes, enjoying the fruits of his garden (hospital) in a very relaxed and stress-free environment.

During this time, I realised that even though I, too, was a practicing chartered accountant like the hospital owner but was involved in taking care of the execution part, dedicating around 15 hours a day to take care of my clients. However, I was neglecting other business aspects, like raising bills to the clients, making collections, meeting new clients, developing new business, and adding new product lines. Because of this, I was not able to scale my business, whereas he was enjoying all the comforts of his life. He was spending only a few hours at the Hospital; he was living a stress-free and relaxed life, and he was able to take his hospital business to a scalable model and was making a lot of money.

At that time, I came to understand the power of delegation of duties. In my 33-year career, I've observed that, much like me, many business owners struggle with knowing how to delegate their powers to their teams and guide them to work cohesively towards the vision and mission of the organisations. Although they have all the dynamism and competence to take their business to the new highs, they often lack the formal knowledge required to develop and nurture the second line of his command team. This team is really important for getting things done and making sure everyone is on the same page with the company's goals. This also lets business owners step back from everyday work and spend more time creating new products and growing the business.

In the next chapter, we will discuss the importance of delegation and how to delegate effectively to bring the desired results from the team and the business.

"

*If you want to do a few small things,
do them yourself. If you want
to achieve great things and make
a significant impact, learn to delegate.*

"

5

DELEGATION OF DUTIES

Delegation enables you to focus on more important tasks or tasks for which you are better suited. The time saved through delegation reduces your pressure and stress. This allows you to concentrate and allocate more time to your most important tasks. Assigning responsibility for a task to your managers not only lightens the load on your shoulders, but also helps your team members grow and develop. When done properly, delegation can have a major positive impact on your team's productivity and motivation. For example, delegating customer service tasks to a subordinate saves you the time that you would otherwise spend interacting with customers and handling issues. Consequently, you would have more time to design products and market them.

Why is delegation important?

Delegation is a crucial skill for business owners to master, as it allows them to efficiently utilize their time and resources while empowering their team members to take on more responsibilities.

There are two key reasons why delegation is important in building a reliable human resources pool. First, it trains employees in skills and experience, actively involving them in decision-making. This training prepares them to take on higher roles, which is essential for their future positions.

Second, senior staff can take on a more active role in strategic aspects by reducing their workload. However, a common tendency among senior staff is not to delegate all tasks and decision-making to their junior staff, resulting in the waste of their time on less important tasks that their subordinates could easily handle.

Not delegating tasks can lead to inefficiency, as senior staff may not always be able to complete tasks as quickly or effectively as someone with specific and defined job responsibilities.

Benefits of Delegation

It is important to note that delegation should be done strategically and in a way that aligns with the goals and objectives of the team. If done incorrectly, delegation could lead to confusion and inefficiency. Delegating strategically is essential to help both yourself and your team success.

As defined above, delegating means entrusting decision-making authority and carrying out certain tasks to lower levels in the organizational hierarchy. However, it's important to note that delegation doesn't involve entirely relinquishing control. Instead, the superior retains final responsibility and takes on a more strategic role.

Delegation is a crucial skill for any business owner or manager. It allows managers to accomplish more in less time and helps develop the skills and abilities of their team members. However, delegation can be challenging, as it requires trust, communication, and a clear understanding of the tasks & goals. Business owners and managers must learn how to effectively delegate.

There can be several reasons why business owners or managers may not delegate tasks, some of which include the following:

- **Lack of trust:** Business owners and managers may not trust their team members to do the job correctly or to make the right decisions.

- **Fear of losing control:** Business owners and managers may fear losing control over the task or the outcome if they delegate it to someone else.

- **Insecurity:** Business owners and managers may feel insecure about team members' abilities and may believe they are the only ones who can do the job correctly.

- **Perfectionism:** Business owners and managers may be perfectionists and may not want to delegate tasks because they believe that no one else can do them as well as they can.

- **Lack of communication:** It is possible that business owners and managers don't communicate effectively with their team members, making it difficult to delegate tasks.

- **Lack of understanding of delegation:** Business owners and managers may need to fully understand the benefits of delegation and learn how to effectively delegate.

- **Lack of time:** Business owners and managers may need more time to train and mentor their team members, making it difficult for them to delegate tasks.

Disadvantages of Not Delegating Tasks

Not delegating tasks can lead to several disadvantages, some of which include the following:

- **Overwork and burnout:** When business owners try to handle everything themselves, they can quickly become overwhelmed and overworked, leading to burnout and negatively affecting their health and well-being.

- **Inefficiency:** Not delegating tasks can lead to inefficiency as business owners may not always be able to complete tasks as quickly or effectively as someone with the specific skills or expertise needed.

- **Lack of growth and development:** When business owners don't delegate tasks, they deprive team members of the opportunity to develop their delegation skills and abilities, which can hinder their growth and the team's overall development.

- **Limited creativity and innovation:** When only one team member is responsible for a task, it restricts the potential for generating new ideas and solutions from other team members.

- **Lack of expertise:** A lack of knowledge in delegation can result in several negative consequences. The team member to whom the task is delegated may need to acquire the necessary knowledge or skills to complete it correctly, which can lead to mistakes or errors.

Business owners need to recognize these reasons, work on overcoming them, and learn how to effectively delegate in order to achieve their goals more efficiently.

How to Delegate Effectively

Delegation is a crucial skill for any business owner or manager. It allows them to accomplish more in less time and helps to develop their team members' skills and abilities. However, delegation can be challenging, and business owners must learn how to effectively delegate.

Tips for Effective Delegation

- **Trust your team members:** One of the essential aspects of delegation is trust. When business owners trust their team members to take on responsibilities, they create an environment where team members feel empowered to take ownership of their work and make decisions.

- **Communicate openly and with clarity:** Open and clear communication is vital for effective delegation. This is important to reduce confusion when subordinates are carrying out delegated roles. The communication should clearly explain the tasks, along with.

- **Timelines and deadlines for task completion:** The communication should also clearly define the specific expectations, explaining the goal, the required outcome, and the desired objective of delegation. It is also essential to ensure that there is open communication and that the delegated team member feels comfortable asking questions or raising concerns. This helps ensure the success of the delegation and the prompt addressing of any issues or concerns.

- **Recognize and reward success:** When team members succeed, the business owners and the managers must recognize and reward their efforts. This recognition can come in the form of bonuses, promotions, or even verbal acknowledgement.

- **Learn from mistakes:** Delegation can be a learning process, and learning from any errors or challenges is essential. By analyzing what went wrong, managers can identify areas for improvement and make changes to their delegation process moving forward.

- **Provide support & resources:** Delegating a task also means providing support and resources to ensure success. This includes everything from training and mentoring to providing access to tools and equipment. Additionally, offer ongoing support and feedback throughout the process to help your team members stay on track and make any necessary adjustments.

- **Monitor Progress and Provide Feedback:** Monitoring progress and providing feedback is an essential part of the delegation process. By keeping an eye on how the task progresses, you can identify any issues or challenges that may arise and provide guidance and support as needed. Additionally, make sure to provide regular feedback, both positive and constructive, to help your team members improve and grow.

Finally, delegation can lead to greater efficiency. Moreover, it can increase motivation, skill development, and the more effective distribution of work across the organization.

> *Measurement Drives Behaviour*
> *Team Don't Do What You Expect*
> *Team Only Does What You Inspect*

6

MONITORING & MEASUREMENTS

No delegation can be effective if it is not monitored and measured periodically. Regular monitoring can make a worker more productive on the job by reducing the number of mistakes made while also allowing for greater, and more efficient use of one's time. Business owners can more easily recognize an employee's positive abilities through monitoring. It allows a business to see a person's leadership abilities and their willingness to go the extra mile for a customer. Companies can highlight a worker's strengths. As a result, team members feel rewarded for their work and more valued by the business owners.

Monitoring not only reduces a worker's mistakes on the job but also identifies fixable workplace problems. Observation allows a company to quickly address an error, preventing the mistake from happening again. Business owners also learn about their own shortcomings through employee monitoring. as well.

Lastly, worker observation increases productivity. Monitoring how workers behave during the workday may reveal attitudes that need to be changed to make people more efficient and safer.

Monitoring and measuring operations and other activities will establish a mechanism to ensure that your organization is meeting its policies, objectives and targets. To meet this requirement, your organization must follow six steps:

1. Identify the processes that have significant impacts and risks.

2. Determine the key characteristics of the activity to be monitored.

3. Select the suitable way to measure the key characteristics.

4. Record data on performance, controls and deliverables, along with objectives and targets.

5. Determine the frequency with which to measure the key characteristics.

6. Establish management review and reporting.

Establishing the monitoring and tracking criteria for each activity that has a significant impact or risk, along with the action plan needed to mitigate those risks, will help you improve the processes, making them more efficient and faster. This will ultimately lead to greater productivity and result in building more capabilities in every division of the organisation.

There can be economy
only where there is efficiency.

OPERATIONAL EXCELLENCE

Monitoring and measuring progress is an essential part of the delegation process. By keeping an eye on progress, you can identify any issues or challenges that may arise and provide guidance and support as needed. Workers are the backbone of any organisation and must be kept happy and motivated. It is a human tendency that if the team is not receiving regular feedback relevant to their work, the team becomes contended and stops improving. That's where feedback comes in. Feedback is a powerful tool that can help you to keep your workers on track and improve their efficiencies and performance. Regular feedback, both positive and constructive, will help your team members improve, grow and work diligently.

The importance of feedback for managers and leaders is well recognized. Providing feedback brings multiple benefits for both teams and managers in terms of their development. It will improve the quality of your work and create a more positive environment within the organisation.

The most critical aspect of gathering feedback is the person who provides it. It is important to choose someone whom you trust and respect. After every feedback session, keep track of the outcomes and learning in a journal or notebook. This practice will help you track your progress, identify potential problems early on, and devise solutions accordingly.

Using this system, you can increase efficiency and improve team cohesion through reliable feedback. The feedback exercise allows team leaders to get to know their team members better and form stronger work relationships. It will also ensure that they have good and thorough knowledge of each team member. Team leaders can also have face-to-face meetings with team members, providing an excellent opportunity for team members to raise issues or concerns. These meetings or sessions allow team leaders to personally discuss individual team members' work, wellness, performance, motivation, team environment, and more. This not only provides team leaders with valuable insights at the ground level but also promotes harmony and cohesiveness among teams within the organisation, working towards the common objective of the organisation and achieving excellence in operations.

*You don't build a business.
You build people,
then people build business.*

~Zig Ziglar

8

BUILD CAPACITIES

Now, let's recap what we have discussed in the previous pages: how a business owner can free himself from day-to-day activities by delegating their duties to team leaders. This allows them to focus on core areas of business development and the creation of business products, which ultimately leads to a well-organised structure of personnel and business growth.

Delegation also facilitates personal development and the growth of team leaders. It is a well-established fact that when the individuals within an organisation grow in terms of skills and abilities, the entire organisation experiences growth. The process of delegation, monitoring and measurements not only improves efficiency but also provides you with the opportunity to scale your business and make your daily work life easier and less stressful. This, in turn, aids you in building capacities within your existing business at no additional costs.

This will serve as the foundation upon which you can enhance your business processes, supporting your journey towards increasing your capacity and in turn giving you more time to further develop your capabilities.

9

BLUE PRINT OF DELEGATION

In this chapter, we will discuss the steps to implementing a system to run our business effectively, seamlessly and frictionless.

1. Organisational Chart:

First of all, you should create an organisational chart of your organisation in detail, clearly defining the roles and responsibilities of each team leader and team member. The organisational chart will provide you with a bird's-eye view of your business, allowing you to identify gaps and avoid duplication of efforts. This will also help business owners identify areas where they are working and require delegation to free themselves from routine tasks, enabling them to spend more time on the strategic aspects of their business where they can add value.

2. Build Cohesive Leadership Team:

Build a leadership team that is passionate, clear and aligned with the organization's goals. They should have a collective sense of ownership for those goals. The team members understand each other's roles and responsibilities and hold each other accountable for the commitments and behaviours. They should regularly engage in productive and constructive criticism.

3. Define Responsibility & Accountability for Teams:

The business owner should clearly define the responsibilities and accountability of each team leader and managers in writing, specifying what is expected from them. This information should be documented so that in the case of any vacancies, the same can be communicated to newly appointed employees by the team leaders.

4. Develop a Business Plan:

The business owner should hold a meeting with team leaders before the start of each financial year to set targets of the upcoming year for each department and create a well-defined business plan to achieve those targets, with the consent of each team leader. During this meeting, they will discuss the challenges and risks involved in achieving the targets and how to mitigate them. This process will help the business owner and team leaders to create a clear picture and roadmap for achieving the targets well in advance. This exercise will provide team leaders with a clear understanding of what is expected from them and how to achieve it. It will also serve as a team-building exercise for the core leadership team, motivating them to work towards achieving the yearly targets.

5. Monthly Meeting of Team Leaders:

The business owner should hold monthly meetings in the first week of each subsequent month to review the previous month's work with all the team leaders together. During these meetings, the team leaders will present a report on the previous month's work of their respective departments, specifying what was expected from them and what they have achieved. This exercise will help them identify gaps and reasons behind them. Discussion will take place among the core team on how to address those gaps. This exercise enables business owners to take timely action to address concerns and ensure that the team is consistently and persistently working towards achieving the set targets.

6. Performance Indicators:

The business owners should establish performance indicators of each team member, which should be well-defined and measurable. The performance of each team member should be evaluated on a weekly basis. The business owner will hold weekly meetings with each team member to review their performance. If there are any gaps between the actual work performed by the team member and what was expected from them, the business owner should analyse the reasons behind it. It is the business owner's responsibility to provide full support and guidance to every team member who is not performing well and to address any gaps that may exist. This assistance helps team members work smoothly and effectively.

7. Minutes of Meetings:

The business should create minutes of every monthly meeting of team leaders, documenting the discussion on core issues, decisions made, and action taken for each concern. The minutes should also outline the responsibilities assigned to the core team for the actions to be taken by them, which will be reviewed in the next meeting. These minutes should be properly documented and stored in a safe place for future references.

10

PREPARING FOR YOUR JOURNEY

The concept of success is simple and easy to understand, and it can be put into practice immediately. The ideas explained in the previous chapters are not new; rather they are a collection of age-old concepts rearranged in a new way. What's different now is that everyone can comprehend and put this plan into action. You have the potential to create your own destiny, but you must discover it.

With the help of this book and the implementation of various processes and practices, you are now well-prepared for your journey in this world. You possess the necessary tools and insights to overcome all obstacles on your path to success. These tools have helped me and other business owners on our journeys. I hope you value and rely on these insights as much as I do. I hope they open doors for you that you never imagined were possible.

You have access to more opportunities than any previous generation. Make the most of these opportunities and take a step closer to your goals each day. Achieving business success is no longer limited to a select few, nor is it ahead of your time. It is no longer an extraordinary feat. It is within the reach for every business owner, as its secrets can now be comprehended. I know you possess the talent to achieve much more.

The time to take action towards building an organization and a cohesive leadership team is now, where everyone collaborates to run the business in a seamless, frictionless, noise-free and stress-free environment.

Creating a stress-free business environment is an ongoing and ever-evolving process. If you would like someone to assist you in implementing the concepts related to a stress-free environment, reach out for a free one-to-one discovery session at:

Gulshan Gaba
Phone: 9810189050
Mail: gulshan@vpgs.in